Canyons

by Alyse Sweeney

Consulting Editor: Gail Saunders-Smith, PhD

Consultant: Nikki Strong, PhD
St. Anthony Falls Laboratory
University of Minnesota

AURORA PUBLIC LIBRARY

CAPSTONE PRESS
a capstone imprint

Pebble Plus is published by Capstone Press,
151 Good Counsel Drive, P.O. Box 669, Mankato, Minnesota 56002.
www.capstonepub.com

032010
005740CGF10

Library of Congress Cataloging-in-Publication Data
Sweeney, Alyse.
 Canyons / by Alyse Sweeney.
  p. cm.—(Pebble plus. Natural wonders)
 Includes bibliographical references and index.
 Summary: "Simple text and full-color photos explain how canyons form and why they are an important
landform"—Provided by publisher.
  ISBN 978-1-4296-5005-2 (library binding)
  ISBN 978-1-4296-5592-7 (paperback)
  1. Canyons—Juvenile literature. I. Title. II. Series.
GB562.S94 2011
551.44'2—dc22   2010002789

Editorial Credits

Katy Kudela, editor; Heidi Thompson, designer; Kelly Garvin, media researcher; Eric Manske, production specialist

Photo Credits

Dreamstime/Atm2003, 1; Demid, 7; Holger Mette, 17; Tomas1111, 9
Fotolia/Katrina Brown, cover
James Brunker/magicalandes.com, 15
Peter Arnold/Masa Ushioda, 5
Seapics/Espen Rekdal, 11; Jon Cornforth, 21
Shutterstock/Alexey Stiop, 13; Duncan Gilbert, 19

Note to Parents and Teachers

The Natural Wonders series supports national geography standards related to the physical
and human characteristics of places. This book describes and illustrates canyons. The images
support early readers in understanding the text. The repetition of words and phrases helps early
readers learn new words. This book also introduces early readers to subject-specific vocabulary
words, which are defined in the Glossary section. Early readers may need assistance to read
some words and to use the Table of Contents, Glossary, Read More, Internet Sites, and Index
sections of the book.

Table of Contents

How a Canyon Forms

Fast moving water cuts

deep paths into rock.

Over time, steep walls form.

It's a canyon stretching

across the land.

Rivers form most canyons.

The water wears away

layers of rock.

Deep canyon paths slowly

carve into the rock.

Glaciers make canyons too.

The hard, moving ice

chips off pieces of rock.

Glaciers shape canyons

in mountain valleys.

Some canyons form

on the ocean floor.

Powerful currents of water,

sand, and mud

carve these deep canyons.

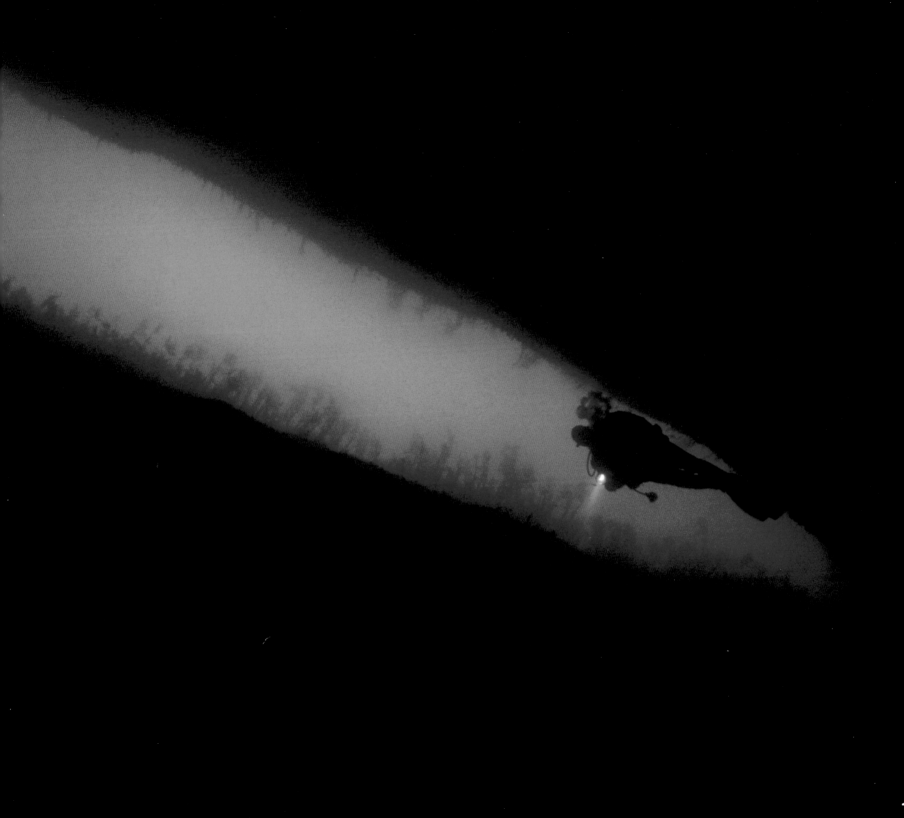

Famous Canyons

Found in Arizona, the

Grand Canyon is 277 miles

(446 kilometers) long.

It is one of the world's

longest canyons.

Peru has one of the world's deepest canyons. Cotahuasi Canyon is 2 miles (3.2 km) deep.

In Jordan, a canyon hides

the ancient city of Petra.

The entrance to the city

is a long, narrow canyon.

People and Canyons

Long ago, people carved homes

into canyon cliffs.

These homes kept them safe

from bad weather

and wild animals.

People carved pictures

on canyon walls.

Today these pictographs

give us clues about

life long ago.

Glossary

current—the movement of water in a river or an ocean

glacier—a large mass or sheet of ice found in high mountains or polar areas

pictograph—a picture used as a symbol in ancient writing systems

valley—an area of low ground between two hills or mountains; rivers and lakes often form in valleys

Read More

Hall, M. C. *Grand Canyon National Park*. Symbols of Freedom. Chicago: Heinemann Library, 2006.

Mis, Melody S. *Exploring Canyons*. Geography Zone: Landforms. New York: PowerKids Press, 2009.

Internet Sites

FactHound offers a safe, fun way to find Internet sites related to this book. All of the sites on FactHound have been researched by our staff.

Here's all you do:

Visit www.facthound.com

FactHound will fetch the best sites for you!

Index

Word Count: 167

Grade: 1

Early-Intervention Level: 22